I Love FASHION

Crazy Colouring for Kids Book 1

First published in 2015 by Kyle Craig Publishing

Text and illustration copyright © 2015 Kyle Craig Publishing

Editor: Alison McNicol

Design: Elizabeth James, Julie Anson, Alison McNicol, Shutterstock, Inc.

ISBN: 978-1-908707-99-4

A CIP record for this book is available from the British Library.

A Kyle Craig Publication

www.kyle-craig.com